bits and pieces

bits and pieces

understanding and building computing devices

irwin math

CHARLES SCRIBNER'S SONS   NEW YORK

640683

I would like to express my thanks to Mr. Hal Keith for his excellent execution of the drawings for this book. I would also like to thank my son Robert and daughter Nicole for helping me to see things from a young person's point of view.

Additional thanks to Mr. Jerry Holzman of the Bronx High School of Science for his comments and suggestions, to my editor, Ms. Clare Costello, for her patience and support, and to IBM Corporation for permission to use the photographs corresponding to figures 1, 4, and 70.

I would also especially like to acknowledge the love, confidence, and inspiration that my wife Ellen has always demonstrated.

I.M.

With fondest memories,
to my father Sol Math,
whose guidance, love, and understanding
have made all the difference

CONTENTS

List of illustrations

foreword

Ever since its introduction into our technologically oriented world, the computer has captured the imagination of youngsters. Computer-controlled games abound, pocket calculators are commonplace, and low-cost minicomputers have become a major industry. Children just into their teens have mastered the complexities of communicating with these electronic marvels, and programming is even being taught on the elementary school level. Technical terms such as hardware, software, bits, and bytes have become part of our language.

But there is a problem: while we have, indeed, made the computer do our bidding, most of us do not have the slightest idea of what goes on behind the fancy front panel. Better and more complex programs are constantly being published, but the way these programs are handled by the machine seems to be of little interest.

Bits and Pieces introduces our computer-oriented population to the wonder of circuits — circuits that at times almost seem to think. The reader will learn about the mechanical, electromechanical, and electronic devices that have contributed to the development of the modern computer.

Experiments and projects in this book use easily obtained, inexpensive materials to demonstrate how machines, reacting to their surroundings, make simple decisions as well as add, subtract, multiply, and divide. Most of the projects are designed to stand by themselves as complete devices or to be interconnected to perform more complex functions, with the result that a clear understanding of just how these functions work is obtained. Several projects result in operating "computers" that can help make a "real-life" decision or solve mathematical problems.

It is the author's hope that *Bits and Pieces* will instill such an appreciation for the modern computer that one's experiences with this amazing device will be ever more enjoyable.

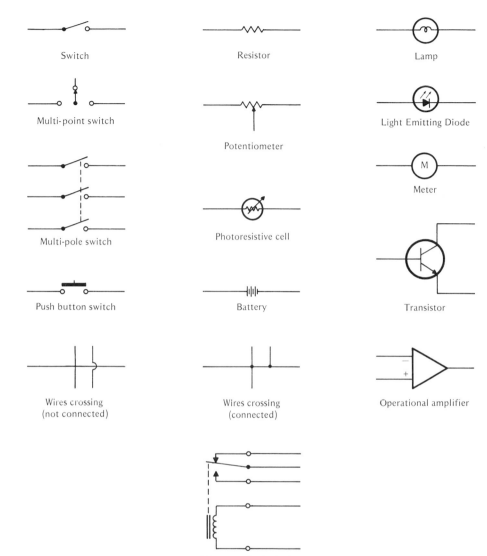

Switch

Resistor

Lamp

Multi-point switch

Potentiometer

Light Emitting Diode

Multi-pole switch

Photoresistive cell

Meter

Push button switch

Battery

Transistor

Wires crossing
(not connected)

Wires crossing
(connected)

Operational amplifier

Electromechanical relay

Electronic symbols used in this book.

CHAPTER 1

EARly COMPUTINg dEVICES

Every time we do work with the aid of a tiny pocket calculator, play a computer-controlled video game, or even glance at a digital watch, we are employing the results of a technology that had its beginning thousands of years ago. The science of counting and computing is about as old as man himself.

Our ancestors used numerous methods to count sheep, baskets of fruit, and populations of tribes. Wooden sticks with notches cut in them, lengths of string with knots, smooth pebbles, and disks of glass and bone abound in the remains of ancient civilizations.

As ancient peoples progressed, their methods of counting and calculating also progressed, leading to the development of the first actual "calculator," the abacus, shown in figure 1. This device, developed sometime before 500 B.C., consists of a series of beads on a wire, which are moved by a skilled operator to perform calculations. Various beads signify units, fives, tens, and so on, and surprisingly high calcu-

1

FIGURE 1

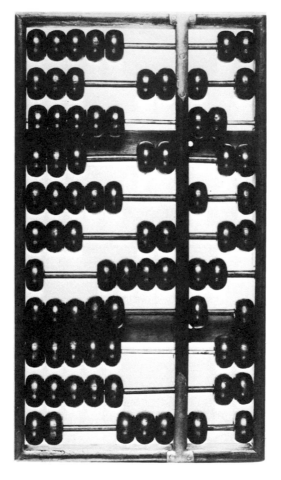

Ancient abacus — the first actual calculator.

lating speeds can be achieved. Although thousands of years old, the abacus is still used in certain parts of the world.

To gain some insight into the operation of the abacus, we can build a simple model to demonstrate how beads can represent numbers. Figure 2 shows all of the construction details. The entire unit should take an hour or so to build. In operation the abacus is oriented

FIGURE 2

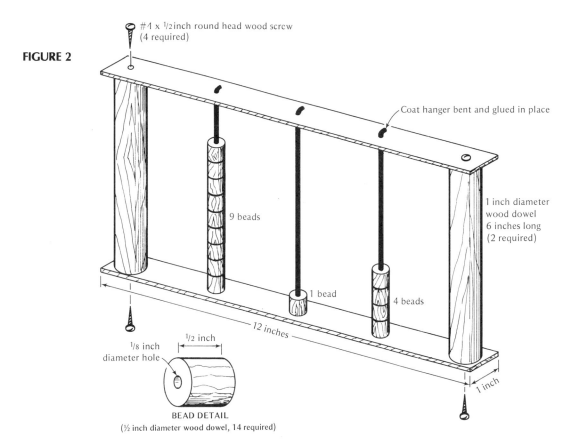

#1 x ½ inch round head wood screw (4 required)

Coat hanger bent and glued in place

9 beads

1 inch diameter wood dowel 6 inches long (2 required)

1 bead

4 beads

12 inches

½ inch

⅛ inch diameter hole

1 inch

BEAD DETAIL
(½ inch diameter wood dowel, 14 required)

Construction details of a simple abacus.

so that the dowels are up and down. All beads are then moved to the right. This signifies 0. To enter a number, move the appropriate beads from right to left. For example, the number 27 would be entered by moving two "tens" beads (20), the "five" bead (5), and two "units" beads (2) to the left. If you now wish to subtract 16, for example, simply move one of the tens beads (10), the five bead (5), and one of the units beads (1) back to the right. You are left with one tens bead (10) and one units bead (1), which equals 11, the answer. Figure 3 shows the manipulations. Although our simple abacus can only count to 99, commercial units can represent numbers into the thousands, and com-

FIGURE 3

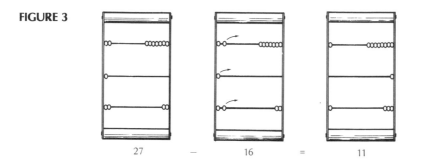

27 — 16 = 11

Subtracting with the simple abacus.

plex calculations take only the time it requires to move the beads.

The first significant step toward creating a true calculator came nearly 2,000 years later, in 1642 in France. The French scientist and philosopher, Blaise Pascal, then a young tax collector trying to simplify his job, built a machine that could add columns of up to eight numbers at once. As shown in figure 4, his device, called "La Pascaline," was actually the forerunner of the modern mechanical counter, best typified by the odometer or mileage counter used in today's automobile

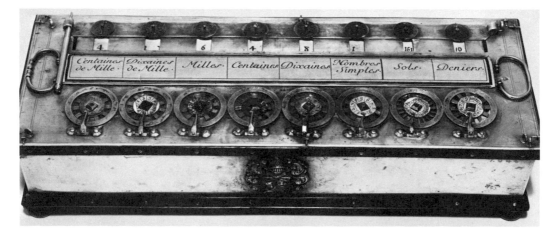

FIGURE 4   *Pascal's "La Pascaline," a calculator built in 1642.*

speedometers. Its basic principle is shown in figure 5. Every time the first wheel (units) passes the number 9, the protrusion advances the next wheel (tens). As the tens wheel passes 90, it, in turn, advances the hundreds column, and so on. Having eight such wheels, La Pascaline could add up to eight-digit sums quickly and accurately.

A number of inventors followed in the footsteps of Pascal, and many mechanical calculating devices were built between 1642 and the early 1900s. In 1822 Charles Babbage built his ''Difference Engine,'' a machine that could solve algebraic equations. Babbage also described, but never actually built, another calculator, which would punch cards and produce a printed record of results in a manner amazingly similar to that of today's machines. Other developments of note were an electrically read punched card system, designed by Dr. Herman Hollevith in 1890; a large analog computer for calculating artillery firing tables, built by Dr. Vannevar Bush in 1925; and a 3,000-relay electromechanical computer, called the Mark 1 Automatic Sequence Controlled Calculator, by Howard Aiden in 1944, which could multiply two 23-digit numbers in 4½ seconds.

The computer age did not really dawn until the announcement of the first true electronic calculator, the ENIAC, developed at the Uni-

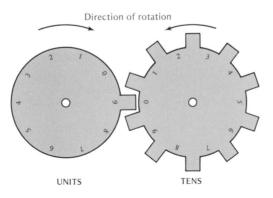

FIGURE 5   *Basic principle of Pascal's calculator.*

versity of Pennsylvania by Drs. J. Presper Eckert, Jr., and John Mauchly in 1946. This huge machine consisted of 18,000 vacuum tubes and over 100,000 related electronic components and weighed over 30 tons, but it embodied circuitry and concepts that are used in computers to this day. Progress was very rapid after ENIAC, and in 1951 many of the same people, led by Eckert and Mauchly, finished work on UNIVAC, the first modern digital computer. This machine was built for the Rand Corporation and was used by the U.S. Census Bureau for their calculations until 1963.

With the advent of the transistor in 1948, and the development of the integrated circuit in the late 1950s and early 1960s, computers and calculators became smaller and smaller, finally culminating in the miniature pocket calculators and desk-type computers of today.

It may be hard to believe, but the simplest four-function calculator ($+$, $-$, $\times$, $\div$) of today is vastly more complex and faster than the giant ENIAC of just a few years ago.

2

Let's get down to basics

Although many people are aware of the ways computers or calculators are used, few have any idea of how the computations are actually done within the machine. Let us begin to gain an understanding of this by considering the two primary ways in which electricity can be made to represent a number.

We should first remember that electrical current can flow only in a complete path or circuit, such as that shown in figure 6. When the switch is closed, the path is complete and the lamp lights. When the switch is opened, the path is broken and the lamp goes out. If the switch were to be quickly opened and closed, bursts or pulses of current would flow and cause the lamp to blink. The number of these blinks or pulses produced per second, for example, could be used to represent a number. Ten pulses per second would represent the number 10, eight pulses the number 8, and so on. By utilizing additional electronic counting circuitry, these pulses could then be processed and

FIGURE 6   *Simple complete circuit to produce digital pulses.*

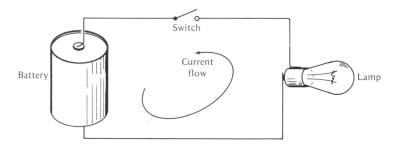

used for calculations of all sorts. This method of representation is called *digital* and always consists of discrete pulses or events, usually related to time. Notches cut in wood, knots tied on a string, and beads on an abacus are all digital representations of numbers.

Figure 7 shows the other primary method of representing numbers, the *analog* method. In this case a battery is connected across a device called a voltage divider. When the arm of the voltage divider is moved to the clockwise (CW) position, all of the battery voltage is connected to the voltmeter. If a ten-volt battery were used in this example, the voltmeter would read ten volts. As the arm is moved away from the CW position toward the counterclockwise (CCW) posi-

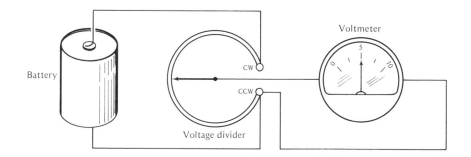

FIGURE 7   *Simple circuit demonstrating analog techniques.*

tion, less and less of the battery voltage is present and the meter reading falls lower and lower. At the halfway point the meter would indicate five volts. When the arm fully reaches the CCW position, the meter indicates zero. If we make the available voltage equal to the number we wish to represent, we have an analog representation of that number. As in the digital method, additional circuitry is used for the actual calculations. Analog representations are always continuous amounts, not necessarily related to time. A thermometer, automobile speedometer, and common ruler are all analog devices.

If one compares digital to analog according to the two previous examples, it appears that many pulses are necessary to represent normal numbers digitally. Decimals and large numbers require more pulses, and it seems that things could get very complicated in short order. An analog system, on the other hand, simply requires that one turn the knob on a voltage divider: the finer the resolution of the divider, the more accurate the number. Decimals in this system are simple to implement.

The analog system would therefore seem to be the more practical, and were it not for the large quantity of microscopic components that can fit into an integrated circuit, and the resulting low cost due to high-volume production, one would be correct in thinking that most computers would be analog in nature. Manufacturing techniques,

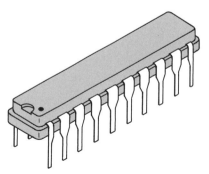

FIGURE 8   *A typical integrated circuit as used in a modern computer.*

FIGURE 9

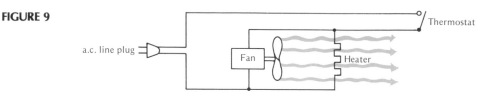

A rudimentary "thinking" circuit.

however, have reduced costs to such an extent that integrated circuits like those shown in figure 8, containing thousands of transistors and related components, cost a couple of dollars, far less than a precision voltage divider. ICs such as these are the backbone of the computer industry today and the reason most modern units are digital in nature.

An interesting question that often arises as one "gets into" computers is whether machines in general can actually think. While at times it certainly seems so, the fact is that any computer, analog or digital, can only react to what the user puts into it — and as the user tells it to react. In this regard, therefore, machines do not really think. As food for thought, however, you might wish to consider the simple circuit in figure 9. This is the circuit of a common heater with a thermostat. As you can see, when the thermostat closes a complete circuit is formed and both the fan and the heating element push warm air into the room. When the temperature of the room rises to some preset level, the thermostat opens and the heat stops. In a way this simple collection of components is (a) noticing the temperature of the room, (b) "remembering" a preset, desired temperature, (c) turning on heat when the room temperature drops below the preset point, and (d) turning off the heat when the temperature reaches the preset point. Does such a device actually "think" on a very rudimentary scale?

In the following chapters of this book we will learn more about analog and digital systems as we build projects that utilize both methods. In some cases these projects will also appear to think. It is interesting to consider just how "intelligent" computing devices actually are.

CHAPTER 3

ANALOG DEVICES

We have already seen, in figure 7, how a number or quantity can be represented by an electrical voltage. Now it is time to look at some of the ways these voltages can be used in simple calculating circuits.

To do so we will require some inexpensive electronic components and batteries, all of which can be easily obtained from a local electronics hobby store or well-equipped TV-stereo repair shop, or even from a cooperative amateur radio operator or electronics experimenter living in the neighborhood. Figure 10 shows these components and their electrical circuit representations. We will use two of the potentiometers or variable resistors, as they are often called, as our number-to-electrical voltage dividers, the batteries and on-off switch as our power source, and the milliampere meter and third potentiometer as our indicator or readout. You should also acquire three large pointer knobs for the potentiometers.

Begin by making a base or ''breadboard'' for our experiments by

FIGURE 10

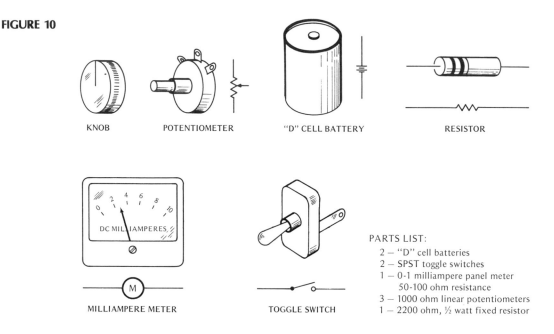

KNOB   POTENTIOMETER   "D" CELL BATTERY   RESISTOR

MILLIAMPERE METER   TOGGLE SWITCH

PARTS LIST:
2 — "D" cell batteries
2 — SPST toggle switches
1 — 0-1 milliampere panel meter
    50-100 ohm resistance
3 — 1000 ohm linear potentiometers
1 — 2200 ohm, ½ watt fixed resistor

Electronic components used in experiments.

obtaining a 12″ length of 1 × 6 pine from the local lumberyard and sanding it smooth on all sides. Now, referring to figure 11, cut the pieces shown from a tin can, using tin-snips or a pair of heavy-duty scissors. If the can is flattened first the task will be easier. Be sure to wear work gloves and be *extremely careful,* as the metal is sharp and you can easily get cut. After making the pieces and carefully drilling the required holes, be certain to remove all sharp edges with sandpaper or a small file. Finally, cut two 2″ diameter circles out of cardboard, label one "A" and the other "B," and punch or cut a ⅜″ diameter hole in the center of each. Referring to figure 12, assemble all components on the breadboard, using #6 × ½″ sheet metal or round head wood screws and the hardware supplied with the various components. Be especially careful that the spacing is correct for the battery holders. Notice that one potentiometer and the meter are not mounted.

FIGURE 11

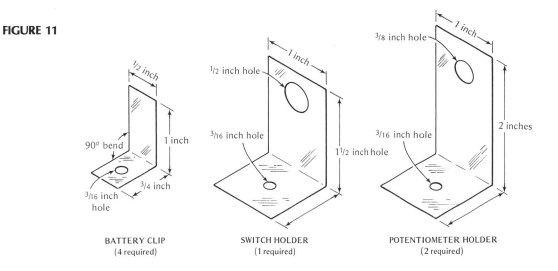

BATTERY CLIP
(4 required)

SWITCH HOLDER
(1 required)

POTENTIOMETER HOLDER
(2 required)

Tin-can metal parts used in experiments.

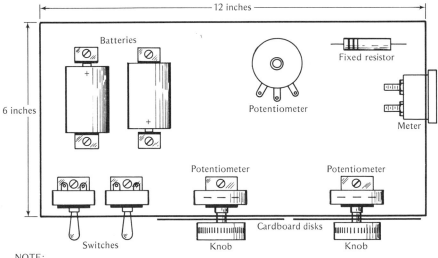

NOTE:
The fixed resistor, meter, and calibration potentiometer are not mounted.

FIGURE 12   *Arrangement of components on the breadboard.*

We are now ready to calibrate the various portions of our calculator. First, the readout: to make matters simple, we will assume that the 0 to 1 scale represents 0 to 10, so that each major division on the scale represents one unit. Connect the meter, the fixed resistor, and its potentiometer, which we will now call the "calibration control," with short lengths of bell wire, as shown in figure 13. Turn the shaft of the control one full clockwise turn. Now connect the battery holders to each other and to the meter by loosening the wood screws and then retightening them with the bell wire pressed between the screw heads and metal. Place the two batteries in their holders and note the deflection of the meter pointer. Slowly turn the calibration shaft counterclockwise until the meter reads exactly 10. The meter is now calibrated, and the calibration potentiometer should not be adjusted further.

Remove the batteries and rewire the circuit as shown in figure 14. Be careful to do the job neatly and correctly. Recheck the wiring two

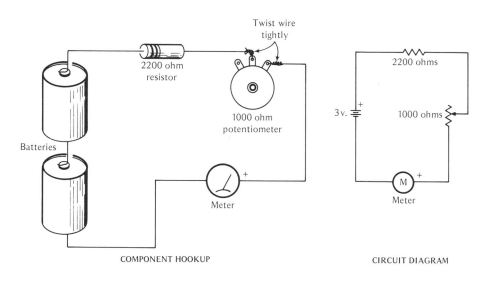

COMPONENT HOOKUP   CIRCUIT DIAGRAM

FIGURE 13   *Calibration circuit for meter.*

FIGURE 14

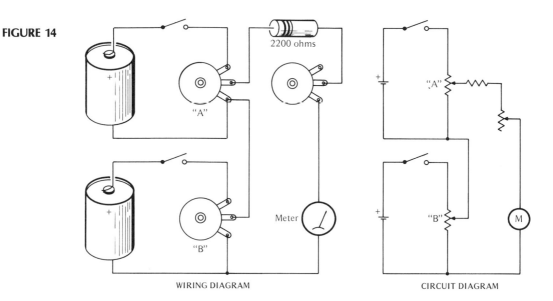

WIRING DIAGRAM   CIRCUIT DIAGRAM

Simple experimental calculator.

or three times to be certain it is correct. When wiring is complete turn the A and B knobs one full counterclockwise turn and, with a felt-tipped marking pen, label the position of the pointer on both knobs 0 on the respective cardboard disks. We will now calibrate the inputs. Place the batteries in their holders with the terminals as shown in the diagram and be sure the switches are in the ON position. Slowly turn the A knob clockwise until the meter reads one major division on its scale. Label this point 1. Continue for 2, 3, and finally 4. Divide the space between the numbers with ¼" increments and turn knob A back to 0. Now repeat the entire procedure with knob B. When you finish your two input dials should look like figure 15.

At this point the calculator is ready to compute. Our simple circuit will add in the form of A + B = C, where C is the meter scale. Set A and B to any two numbers, and the meter will indicate the sum. Depending on how carefully you calibrated the input dials, fractional numbers such as 1¼ + 2½ are easily handled. For best battery life, turn off the switches when not using the circuit.

FIGURE 15

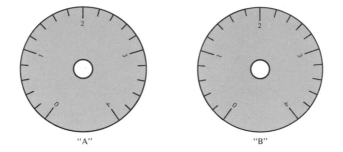

"A"   "B"

The completed calculator dials.

By this time it should be obvious that our calculator is simply adding two voltages together, which is exactly what an analog computer does. It should also be obvious that by adding more battery-potentiometer combinations any amount of numbers can be added. Also, if one were to insert the B input battery backwards, the calculator would now perform A − B = C, or subtraction. In the case of subtraction, A must, of course, always be larger than B. Try this and, if you wish, obtain a DPDT toggle switch and connect it as shown in figure 16 to enable your calculator to add or subtract at the flick of a switch.

Commercial analog computing circuits do not use dozens of bat-

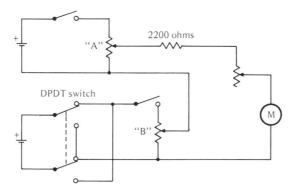

FIGURE 16   *Adding subtraction to the simple calculator.*

FIGURE 17

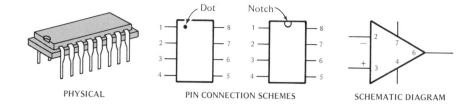

PHYSICAL   PIN CONNECTION SCHEMES   SCHEMATIC DIAGRAM

Typical operational amplifier.

teries but rather a special type of circuit called an operational amplifier, which allows multiplication and division to be performed as well as addition and subtraction. First described in 1947 by John Pagazini and published in 1962 by G.A. Philbrick, the operational amplifier or op-amp, as it is commonly called, is available in integrated-circuit form today and is easy to experiment with. The same electronics parts store from which you obtained the calculator components will usually have these in stock. You should purchase an LM741 or UA741 type, plus a matching socket. If possible, get a so-called wire-wrap socket, as it is easier to work with. The cost of both will be about a dollar. Next obtain a 100,000-ohm linear potentiometer, a 10,000-ohm linear potentiometer, a 10,000-ohm fixed resistor, two nine-volt transistor radio batteries, and holders or clips for the batteries. Figure 17 shows what a typical op-amp looks like, its electrical schematic diagram symbol, and its pin connection numbering scheme.

The classical op-amp circuit, shown in figure 18, owes much of its

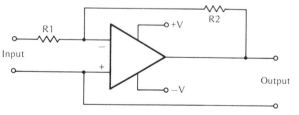

FIGURE 18   *Classical op-amp circuit.*

versatility to the fact that the ratio of two resistances, R1 and R2, determines what happens to the input and output. In the circuit shown the output is equal to the input multiplied by R2/R1. If R2 = R1, then the input equals the output. If R2 is 100,000 ohms and R1/R2 equals 10,000 ohms, then R2 = 10 and the output is ten times the input. If the situation is reversed, and R2 = 10,000 ohms while R1 = 100,000 ohms, then R2/R1 = 0 and the output is 1/10 of the input.

Let us now rewire our breadboard (figure 19) so we can work with an op-amp. Note that the operational amplifier requires some operating power, which is derived from the nine-volt transistor radio batteries. You will have to make cardboard dials and mounting brackets for the two new potentiometers. Remember to exercise care when cutting the tin can metal for the brackets. When rewiring is complete plug the op-amp into its socket and turn both potentiometers one full counterclockwise turn. Mark this point on R2, the 100,000-ohm potentiometer dial, 0. The 10,000-ohm dial will be calibrated later. Turn on the switch and connect the batteries, making sure + and − are connected correctly. As you would assume, the meter will read 0. Turn input A to 1 and slowly increase R2 until the meter reads 1. Mark this point as 1 on the R2 dial and repeat until you reach 8. We cannot exceed eight volts at the output because the power source to the op-amp is only nine volts. We have now connected the op-amp as a multiplier. If you turn the A and R2 knobs to various positions you will see that the meter indicates A × R2, as long as the answer does not exceed 8.

To connect the circuit to one that can divide, turn off the power, disconnect the batteries, and interchange the 100,000-ohm potentiometer and the 10,000-ohm potentiometer. Replace the old cardboard dial on the 100,000-ohm potentiometer with a new blank one and make sure the 10,000-ohm potentiometer is still set fully clockwise. Mark the latter's dial 1. Now apply power, set A to 4, and turn the 10,000-ohm potentiometer until the meter reads 2. Mark this point 2 on the new dial. Continue turning the knob until the meter reads 1 and ⅓. Mark this point 3. Finally, repeat for a meter reading of 1 and mark this point 1. When this is done you may set A to any number and R2 to 2, 3, or 4. The meter will indicate the quotient of A divided by R2.

Last, but by no means least, let us see how an op-amp can add and subtract. Again, rewire your breadboard so that it matches figure 20. Turn both 1,000-ohm input potentiometers to 4 and the 10,000-ohm potentiometer (R2) until the meter indicates 8. When this is done A and B can be set to any numbers and the meter will indicate the sum

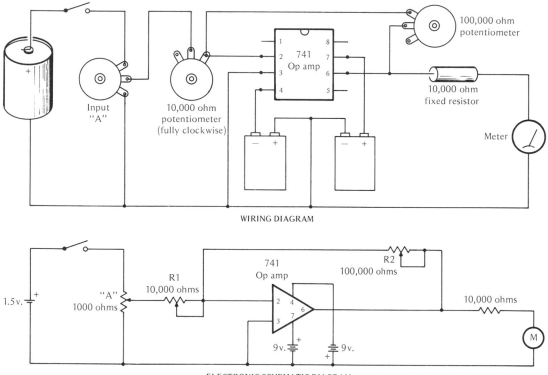

WIRING DIAGRAM

ELECTRONIC SCHEMATIC DIAGRAM

FIGURE 19   *Wiring diagram to multiply with an op-amp.*

of A + B. Reversing the battery polarity of the B input will convert the circuit to one that indicates A − B. A must, of course, be greater than B.

When you have tried the various circuits and procedures that have been described, you should have a bit of an understanding of how electronic components can manipulate voltages to do arithmetic problems. An exact description of what goes on inside the op-amp is beyond the scope of this book, but the results of using this component are quite easy to see. In industry op-amps similar to the 741 are employed in a myriad of applications where analog quantities must be measured and processed. While the circuits employed are usually more complex, the basic ideas are the same. The operational amplifier, therefore, has become one of the major building blocks of analog computing circuitry.

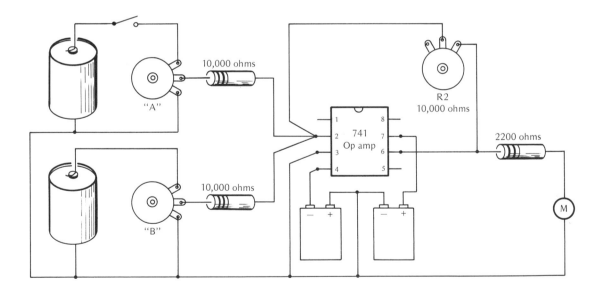

FIGURE 20   *Op-amp circuit to add two numbers.*

CHAPTER 4

AN ANALOG COMPUTER

With some understanding of analog principles and the operational amplifier, we can proceed to build a practical device that will do useful calculations. Figure 21 is a drawing of our analog computer, and figure 22 is the electrical schematic diagram and parts list, many items on which you already have from past experiments. This computer will add, subtract, multiply, and divide and, if built and calibrated carefully, will give answers that are accurate to 5% or better.

When you examine the diagram, you will see that the "A" and "B" inputs are voltage divider potentiometers as before, connected to an operational amplifier in a circuit that either adds or subtracts, depending on the position of switch S4. The output of the op-amp, therefore, will be a voltage corresponding to $\dfrac{A + B}{2}$ or $\dfrac{A - B}{2}$ (notice the values of R1, R2, and R3). This output is applied to one side of our meter, while the other side of the meter is connected to another potentiometer, which can be set to any value from 0 to the equivalent

FIGURE 21

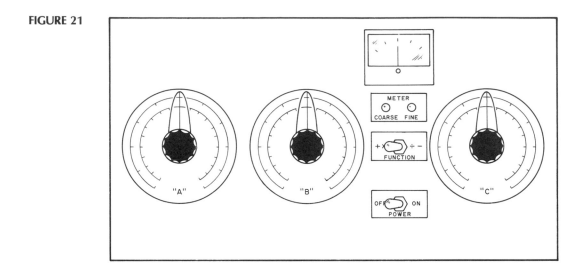

Drawing of analog computer.

of A + B or the full available voltage. If the voltage applied to both sides of the meter is equal, which occurs when the potentiometer is set to the same value as the output of the op-amp, the meter will read 0. When it is not, the meter will deflect either upscale or downscale. We will call this third potentiometer "C," and *it* will be our new read-out. The meter will only be used to tell when C is at the correct position. Instead of trying to obtain answers on a tiny, cramped meter scale, we can now read them on a large, easy-to-read dial. We have also added two pushbutton switches to give us high and low sensitivity positions of the meter, which will make adjusting C much easier. The way these switches are used will be described later.

Since the circuit will add and subtract A and B, how can it multiply and divide, you may ask? To do this we employ the mathematical fact that the sum of the logarithms of two numbers is equal to the logarithm of the product of the numbers. Without a long explanation of logarithms, this simply means that if we supply two sets of scales for A, B, and C, one linear and one logarithmic, we can add and subtract with

FIGURE 22

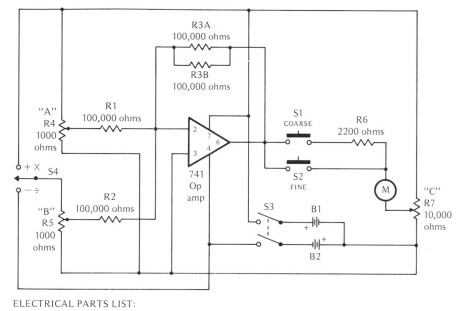

ELECTRICAL PARTS LIST:

M = 0-1 milliampere meter (0 center preferred)
R1, R2, R3A, R3B = 100,000 ohms, 5%, ½ watt resistor
R4, R5 = 1000 ohms linear potentiometer
R6 = 2200 ohms, 5%, ½ watt resistor
R7 = 10,000 ohms linear potentiometer
S1, S2 = SPST normally open push button switch
S3 = DPDT toggle switch
S4 = SPDT toggle switch
B1, B2 = 6v. lantern batteries
μA741 or LM741 = Operational amplifier

Electrical schematic diagram of analog computer.

the linear scales and multiply and divide with the log scales. This procedure is well known to users of the somewhat dated slide rule so popular in the 1940s and 1950s.

Begin construction with the cabinet. Figure 23 shows the details. All materials can usually be obtained from the scrap bin at the local lumberyard. As this is a project that you will probably want to use and show off many times, take care in its construction. You might wish to

stain the wood and then add a coat of shellac, varnish, or polyure-
thane for appearance.

Next prepare the three dials for A, B, and C. Figure 24 shows the
linear and logarithmic scales for the dials, which are exactly the same
for A and B. The C dial is shown in figure 25. All dials are shown full
size and should be copied from the drawing on tracing paper and then
attached with rubber cement to 4″ diameter cardboard or posterboard disks. Try to copy the dials as carefully, neatly, and accurately
as possible, as they are directly related to the accuracy of the computer. (The use of a photocopy machine may help in this procedure.)
Make the COARSE/FINE label and function switch label as per figure
26. When the cabinet, dials, and labels are completed, mount all front
panel controls. Secure the dials and labels to the front panel with the
appropriate control hardware and rubber cement, respectively.

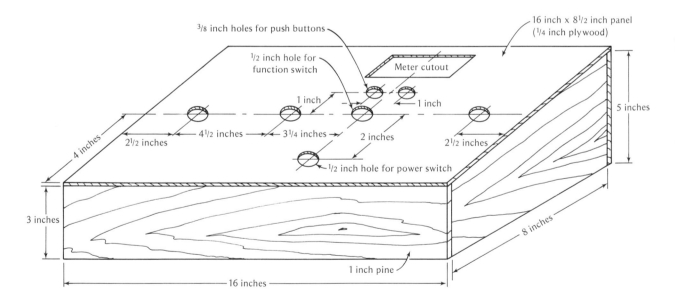

FIGURE 23   *Cabinet for analog computer.*

FIGURE 24

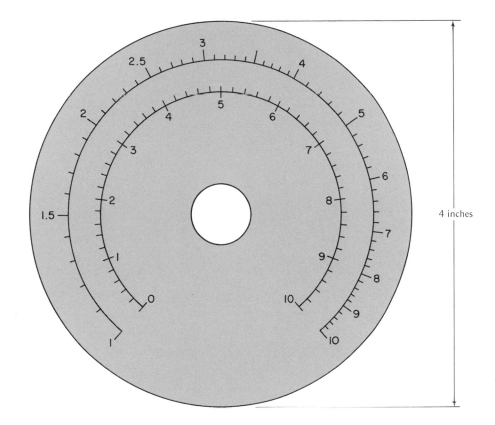

4 inches

Full-size dial for "A" and "B."

Referring to figure 27, begin to wire the computer. Follow the pictorial diagram and make sure that all connections are made properly. Be especially certain that the function switch (S4) is connected correctly. When you have completed this stage, prepare three indicator knobs as shown in figure 28. Cut the pointers from thin, clear plastic, such as the type used by some manufacturers for collar stays in new shirt packages, often available free from a clothing dealer, or thin "five to ten mil" acetate, which you can get at an art supply store. After

FIGURE 25

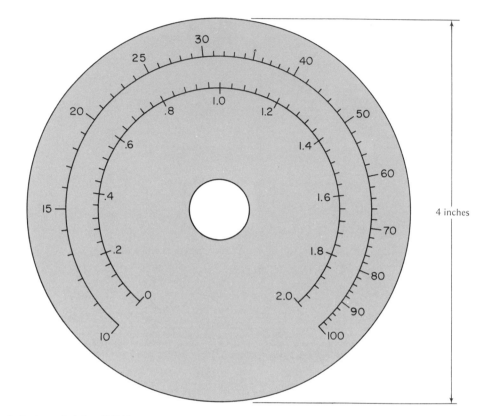

Full-size dial for "C."

cutting, scratch a "hairline" with a pin or needle and rub some ink into the scratch with your finger. Then glue the pointer onto the knob as shown. To align the pointers properly, turn the A, B, and C potentiometers counterclockwise all the way. Push the knob-pointer assemblies onto the shafts of the proper potentiometers and turn counterclockwise until the hairlines are over the 0 marks on the linear scale. Now tighten the setscrews to hold the knobs in place. You should be able to set the pointers to any number between 0 and 10. If either 0 or 10 is not exactly at opposite ends of the rotation of the knobs,

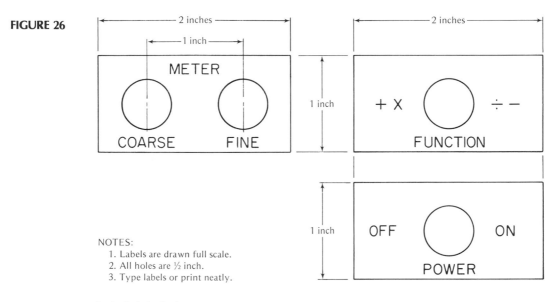

FIGURE 26

METER

COARSE   FINE

FUNCTION

+ X   ÷ −

POWER

OFF   ON

NOTES:
  1. Labels are drawn full scale.
  2. All holes are ½ inch.
  3. Type labels or print neatly.

Switch labels for computer.

slightly adjust the setscrews until you get them as close to equal as possible.

At this point you are ready to test the computer. With the power switch in the OFF position, connect the two lantern batteries and perform the following steps:

1. Turn all potentiometers fully counterclockwise to 0.
2. If you are not using the optional zero-center meter, offset the meter you do have for easier reading by turning the zero-adjust screw until the pointer moves one division or more away from 0. This new position will be our 0.
3. Set the function switch to +X and use the linear scale.
4. Push the COARSE then the FINE pushbuttons. The meter should continue to read 0.
5. Set A and B to 10 and push the COARSE pushbutton. The meter should deflect upscale.

FIGURE 27

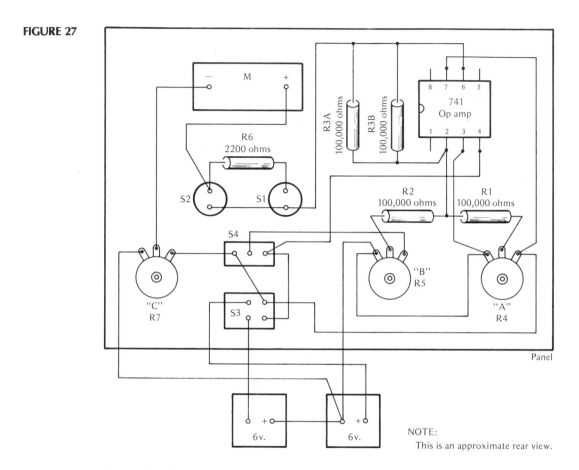

Pictorial wiring diagram of computer.

6. Continue to push the COARSE button while you turn the C dial toward 10. The meter pointer should slowly move toward 0 and should read 0 when C points to 20.
7. Now turn both A and B to 5. Push COARSE and turn C until the meter reads 0. This point should be 10 on C.
8. By pushing the FINE pushbutton, you can make the meter more sen-

FIGURE 28

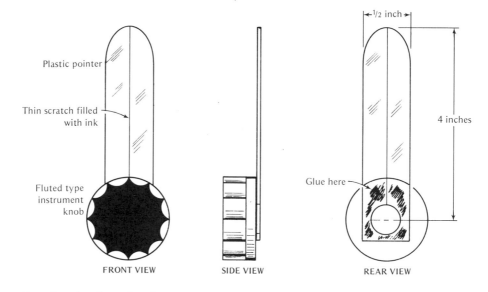

Plastic pointer

Thin scratch filled with ink

Fluted type instrument knob

1/2 inch

4 inches

Glue here

FRONT VIEW   SIDE VIEW   REAR VIEW

Details of pointer knobs.

sitive, thereby allowing a finer adjustment of C. Try this while slowly moving C to either side of the correct answer.

9. If all of the above is correct, the computer is ready for use. If not, readjust the pointers on A, B, and C so that steps 6 and 7 are as accurate as possible. If you get no indications at all, or no 0 readings on the meter, carefully recheck all wiring and, finally, the condition of the batteries.

To add using the computer, set the FUNCTION switch to +X and A and B to the two numbers on the linear scales you wish to add. Push the COARSE button and adjust C for the answer on its linear scale. When you are close to the answer, push the FINE button to set C exactly.

To subtract, set the FUNCTION switch to − ÷ and repeat the above procedure. Remember, A must be larger than B or you will not get an answer. Again, use the linear scales.

Multiplying and dividing are done in the same way except that the log scales are used. The computer will perform all the difficult parts of the mathematics, but you will have to remember where the decimal points or the zeros go. If you wish to add 25 and 40, for example, set A to 2.5 and B to 4.0. The answer, on C, will be 6.5, but if you move decimals in your head you will know that $25 + 40 = 65$. This is all there is to it. After a few problems you will have no trouble carrying out the mental arithmetic.

The operation of our analog computer is very similar to that of the old-fashioned slide rule that was once the mainstay of engineering. If you wish to obtain a book from the library describing these devices, you will learn how to add trigonometric markings to your dials and will gain more insight into solving equations by the analog method. By doing so your analog computer will become a useful tool both for practical applications and as an introduction into actual electronic computing. It is, of course, the first computer that you do truly understand.

CHAPTER 5

building AN ANALOG decision MAKER

In the last chapter we saw how electronic components can be connected to convert numbers to voltages and then used those voltages to solve arithmetic problems. The same components can be used to do other things as well, such as making decisions — one of the major uses of analog circuitry in industry today. To see how this is possible, we will build a device to help us make complex personal decisions in a logical manner similar to the way in which a person might make an actual decision.

Our decision maker is based on the op-amp circuit of figure 29. As you will remember from chapter 3, the operational amplifier will sum the inputs applied to it. This is true even if there are many inputs and whether those inputs are + or −. In figure 29, for example, the output might be A + B + C − D − E.

With this idea in mind, let us now look at the process you might use to make a real-life decision on such a question as "Should I study

FIGURE 29

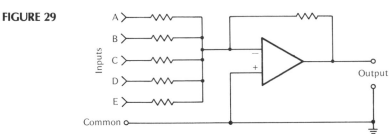

Operational amplifier summer.

for my social studies test tonight when my friend has invited me to a great party?'' This is a difficult decision. You might consider such matters as the following:

1. I know most of the work, so I really don't need much studying.
2. My marks are not that great, so a good grade would help.
3. My parents would disapprove if I didn't study.
4. The party will be great.
5. My friend might get angry if I don't go.

   The reasons for or against going are many, and some are more important than others. What you usually wind up doing is considering all aspects and reaching a decision. The circuit in figure 30 will help you do this with cold electronic logic.
   As you can see, we have connected ten potentiometers to an op-amp. Each of these will be for one factor in the making of our final decision. Furthermore, each potentiometer is connected between a + and − voltage source, thereby allowing the particular factor to be set with varying degrees of yes, no, or maybe (at 0). When all yeses and nos are entered − some of which are more strongly yes or no − the op-amp will tabulate everything and come up with a yes or no final decision. Due to the current drain of ten potentiometers, D cells are used

FIGURE 30

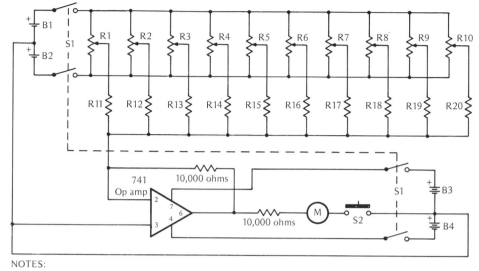

NOTES:
R1 to R10 = 1000 ohm linear potentiometers
R11 to R20 = 10,000 ohm, 5%, ½ w. resistors
S1 = 4P DT toggle switch or 4P 2 position rotary switch
S2 = Normally open push button switch
B1, B2 = 1.5 v. "D" cell batteries
B3, B4 = 9 v. transistor radio battery
M = 1 milliampere (0 center meter)

Analog decision maker schematic diagram.

for the inputs while low-cost transistor radio batteries power the op-amp. The four-pole switch turns everything on and off.

Figure 31 shows the construction details of the housing for the analog decision maker, which should pose no construction problems. Figure 32 shows details of the type of dial and knob needed for the unit. As in the case of the analog computer, dials should be made on posterboard. The meter can be a zero-center type or offset standard unit.

When wiring is completed check all connections a second time and connect the batteries. Make sure +'s and −'s are correct. Calibration of the decision maker is quite simple. First rotate each of the ten factor knobs between full clockwise and counterclockwise to be certain that the dials are properly centered mechanically. Next set all ten dials to 0 and push the decision button. The meter should remain

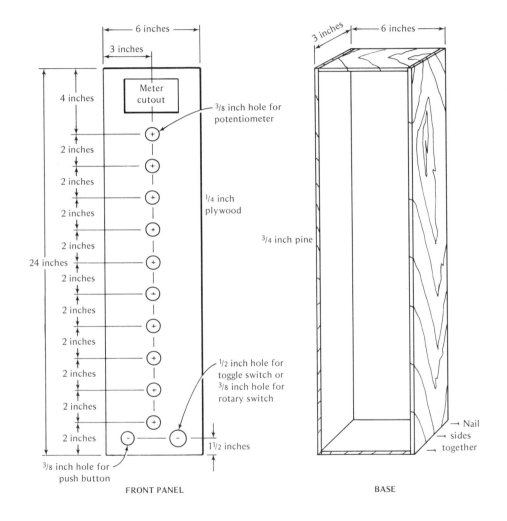

FIGURE 31   *Housing details for decision maker.*

FIGURE 32

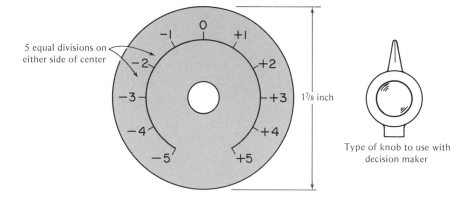

5 equal divisions on either side of center

$1\frac{7}{8}$ inch

Type of knob to use with decision maker

Decision-maker dials and knobs.

at 0. If it deflects toward yes or no, turn each of the ten knobs a tiny distance around 0 to determine which knob is off. When you find the culprit, readjust the knob. With all knobs set at 0, the meter should not deflect when the decision button is pressed.

Once the decision maker is calibrated, you are ready to use it. When you have a problem that calls for using the machine, the procedure is to break it down first into ten smaller, simpler decisions, as in the example at the beginning of this chapter. As you make these decisions, enter the results on the dials. A setting of +5 or −5 indicates a strong yes or no. Intermediate settings are lesser degrees of yes or no, and 0 means maybe. If you have less than ten factors, set the unused knobs to 0. You can vary these settings as much as you wish and reconsider the degrees of yes or no you have entered. Once you push the button, however, all of the inputs you have entered will be processed and the final decision revealed. It is important to note that if you have been honest in making the intermediate decisions, the main decision is really the correct one since it is based upon information that you yourself provided.

Such a device as this analog decision maker is interesting since it not only gives the user some insight into the mature decision-making process but also shows how electronics can be used to reach decisions in industry. For example, each of the inputs could be a different step in an industrial process, such as the mixing of chemicals, matching of dyes for coloring cloth, or, when computing a course for an airplane.

CHAPTER 6

Logical circuits

Up to this point we have dealt with analog circuitry and how varying voltages can be used for computations and even decision making. Now it is time to consider the digital approach. Unlike analog circuits, digital circuits respond only to one of two conditions — the presence of a fixed voltage or current, referred to as logical "1," and the absence of voltage or current, referred to as logical "0." Figure 33 shows, in a simplified manner, how this is accomplished. When a switch is closed, current can flow and the appropriate lamp lights, signifying a 1. When the switch is open, there is no current flow and the output is a logical 0. If each of the lamps has the value shown in the diagram, all numbers from 0 (no lamps lit) to 15 (all lamps lit) can be produced by proper manipulation of the switches. In digital circuitry each piece of information, as represented by a lamp in figure 33, is called a bit. To indicate numbers larger than 15 would require more bits. Since each bit is a factor of 2, doubling the number of bits from

FIGURE 33

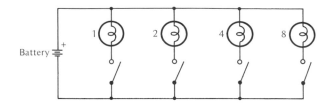

Digital representation of numbers.

four to eight only increases the numbers that can be produced to 255. It is obvious that a great many bits are necessary to represent large numbers. The tremendous complexity of integrated circuits, however, allows thousands and thousands of bits to be handled by rather small components, so this is not a problem. Some integrated circuit chips, such as the one shown in figure 8, for example, can handle 16,000 bits.

Since the operating speed of modern computers is in the range of millions of bits per second, time is not a problem either. Furthermore, as calibration is unnecessary (the circuits respond only to a 1 or 0) very high accuracy can be achieved by simply using more and more bits. This is why most computers and calculators are digital in nature.

As digital computing requires the manipulation of bits, we must look at a family of circuits specifically designed to do this job. These circuits are called digital logic circuits and respond to 0 and 1 inputs by producing 0 and 1 outputs in a relationship that depends on the particular circuit. Demonstrating how these logic circuits work requires that you know how a transistor can be used as a switch. Figure 34 shows this. What you must realize from this drawing is that when a 1 is applied to the base, the collector-to-emitter path conducts. When a 0 is applied, it does not.

With an expenditure of a couple of dollars, we can build and investigate the more common digital logic circuits. You will require some #4 × ½" wood screws; two general-purpose NPN transistors such as the 2N4124, 2N2222, or 2N3904; a silicon diode such as a

FIGURE 34

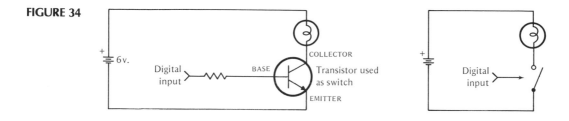

Transistor used as a switch and equivalent circuit.

1N4002; two normally open pushbutton switches; one 330-ohm and two 10,000-ohm fixed resistors; a six-volt lantern battery; and one general-purpose light-emitting diode (LED) as an output indicator. The local electronics parts store will have all of these and, in addition, you will need a simple breadboard, as shown in figure 35. As in the past, exercise care when cutting the tin can metal. When the breadboard is complete, each of the logic circuits should be built and operated as they are discussed.

Now let us look at the first logic circuit, the OR gate. This is shown in figure 36, along with the symbolic logic representation. The function of an OR gate is to produce a 1 output when any one of two inputs is 1. In other words a 1 input to A *or* B will result in a 1 output. As you can see from the circuit, the input to both transistors is 0 when neither of the buttons is pressed. Since the circuits do not conduct, the LED does not light, signifying a 0 output. Pressing either button causes the respective transistor to conduct and the LED to light, indicating a 1 output. By the way, the purpose of the 330-ohm resistor is to limit current flow to proper levels for the LED indicator.

The next logic circuit is the AND gate. This is shown in figure 37, along with the logic representation. The function of an AND gate is to produce a 1 output when both of two inputs are 1. In other words a 1 input to A *and* B will result in a 1 output. As you can see from the circuit, both transistors must conduct in order for the LED to light, so you must press both buttons to produce a 1 output.

In practice the most common logic gates in use are variations of the OR and AND circuits. These are called NOR and NAND circuits and are the same as the OR and AND, but with a logic inversion. Figure 38 should clarify this. The circuit shown is a NOR gate. You will notice that with both inputs at 0, the LED lights. Making either input 1 shunts

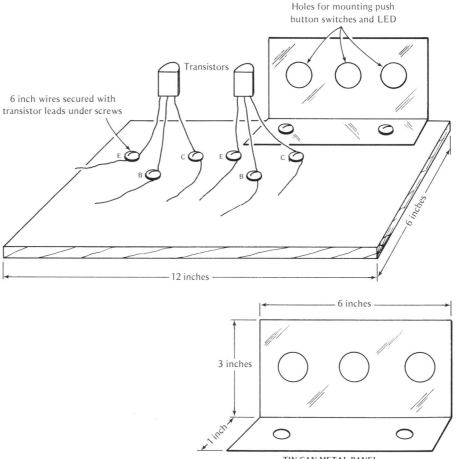

Holes for mounting push button switches and LED

Transistors

6 inch wires secured with transistor leads under screws

E
C
B
E
C
B

6 inches

12 inches

6 inches

3 inches

1 inch

TIN CAN METAL PANEL

FIGURE 35   *Digital circuit breadboard.*

FIGURE 36

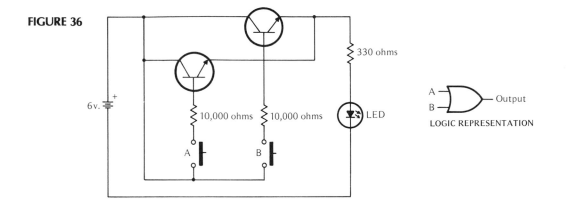

Circuit for OR gate example.

the current flow into one of the transistors, causing the LED to go off. The function of a NOR gate, therefore, is to produce a 0 output when either input is 1. Similarly, a NAND gate will produce a 0 output when both inputs are 1. This is shown in figure 39.

The final logic circuit to be described is the simple inverter. Figure 40 shows the circuit and the logic representation. When the button is not pressed, the input to the transistor is 0. Since the transistor does not conduct, current flows through the 330-ohm collector resistor into

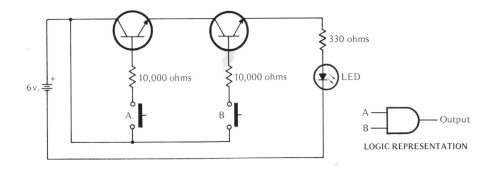

FIGURE 37 *Circuit for AND gate example.*

FIGURE 38

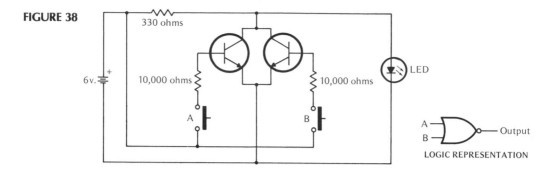

Circuit for NOR gate example.

FIGURE 39   Circuit for NAND gate example.

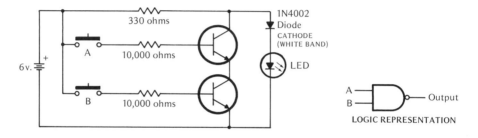

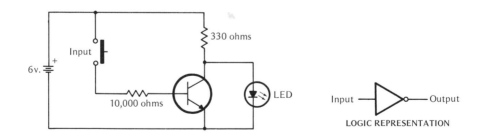

FIGURE 40   Circuit for inverter.

the LED, which lights, indicating a 1. Pressing the button changes the input to a 1, making the transistor conduct. This causes the current to flow through the transistor, so the lamp goes off. The output is now 0.

Figure 41 is a review of the major digital logic circuits and their truth tables. These tables tell, in simple form, how each of the circuits operates.

In a more sophisticated digital computer, many logic circuits such as these are connected to move bits around and perform calculations. In chapter 7 we will look at some practical examples of these circuits.

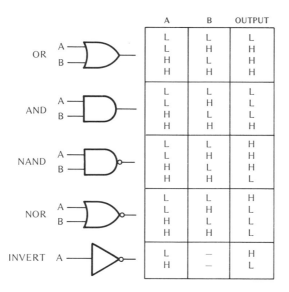

	A	B	OUTPUT
OR	L	L	L
	L	H	H
	H	L	H
	H	H	H
AND	L	L	L
	L	H	L
	H	L	L
	H	H	H
NAND	L	L	H
	L	H	H
	H	L	H
	H	H	L
NOR	L	L	H
	L	H	L
	H	L	L
	H	H	L
INVERT	L	—	H
	H	—	L

FIGURE 41   *Truth table for common logic elements.*

CHAPTER 7

diqital devices

As already mentioned, a computer calculates by manipulating bits, which represent numbers, and logic circuits to come up with the correct answers. Since many bits are actually used, it is difficult for the experimenter to build a practical digital computer. However, a simple adder can be built to show how these circuits work in combination with each other. The logic diagram of this calculation is shown in figure 42. Yet this device can only add two numbers, 1 or 2, together. It is obvious, when you understand how it works, that this could be expanded. Number inputs to our digital calculator are pushbuttons; outputs are LEDs. AND and OR gates are used to do the manipulations.

When you add 1 + 1, AND gate A1 produces an output that lights the 2 LED. Adding 1 + 2 activates AND gate A2 and is applied to the OR gate. Since either input to the OR gate will result in an output, the 3 LED lights. Adding 2 + 2 activates A3, lighting the 4 LED. When you now add the last combination, 2 + 1, A4 is activated and, via the OR

FIGURE 42

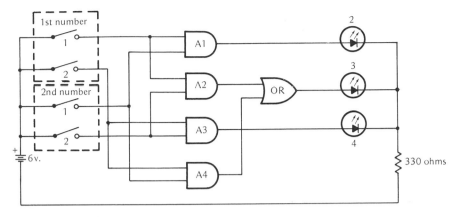

Simple digital adder.

gate, results in an output of 3. If you wish to build a model of this calculator, figure 43 shows the complete circuit. All components are the same as those used in the preceding chapters.

While adding 1 + 2 is not exactly the most interesting achievement in the world, it does illustrate how precise, noncalibrated digital circuits work. Figure 44 represents a more useful device, a digital squarer. Most students know that to square a number you simply multiply the number by itself. Our digital squarer does this for you instantly. Again, in the interest of simplicity, only the numbers from 1 to 10 are used. In this example silicon diodes are used as OR gates. To understand how the circuit operates, look at the number 4, whose square is 16. You will see that the output of the 4 input button is directed to both the 1 OR gate and the 6 OR gate. Since the diodes in these gates only conduct in one direction, from + to −, as shown, only the correct LED lights. Diode OR gates are often used in computing circuitry, since in such applications they are much simpler than the transistor version in figure 36. If you build the circuit in figure 44, be sure to press only one input at a time. Figure 45 shows construction details.

Another digital circuit even more useful than the squarer is the circuit in figure 46. Utilizing diode OR gates, this circuit computes pow-

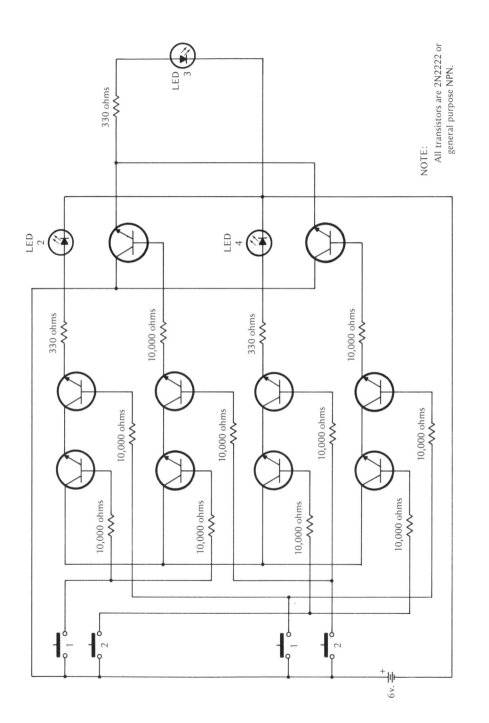

FIGURE 43   *Complete circuit for adder.*

46

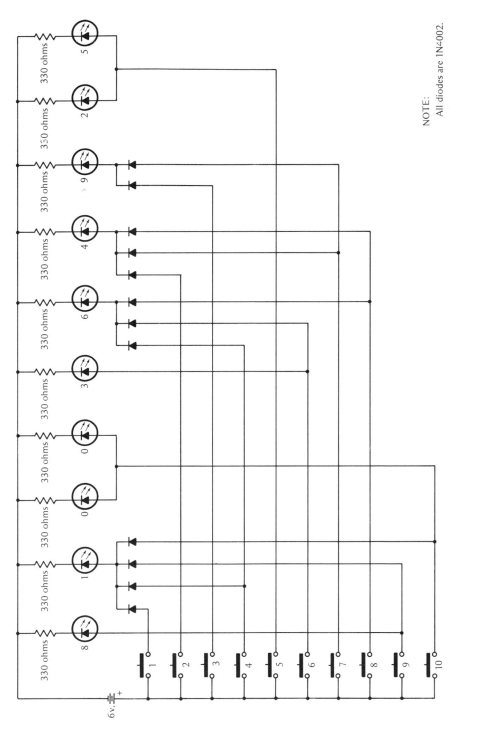

FIGURE 44 Circuit diagram of digital squarer.

NOTE:

All diodes are 1N4002.

FIGURE 45

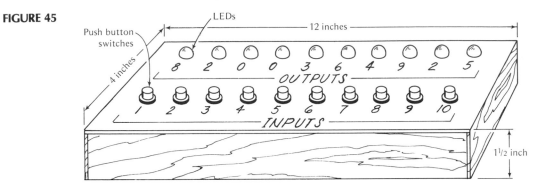

Construction details of squarer.

ers of 2 instantly. The principle of operation is the same as that of the squarer. Again, each "answer LED" is connected to the output of an OR gate and lights when the correct inputs are present. Construction details for this circuit are similar to those in figure 45, except for the input and output labels, for which you should refer to the circuit diagram. Once you understand the principle behind the squarer and powers-of-2 calculator, you can easily design similar circuits to calculate such values as square roots, powers of 3, cube roots, and so on.

It is important to realize that by wiring the preceding circuits you are programming the computer in a manner similar to that in which a larger computer is programmed. Although you are not typing information into a keyboard, you are, for example, "telling" the circuit in figure 46 to light the #6 answer LED only if a 2^4, 2^6, or 2^8 input is present. When you reach Chapter 10, you will see how actual computer programming is similar to this approach.

In addition to calculation, logic circuits can be used for record keeping. In a manner similar to that in the previous example, we can design a digital "memory" that will "remember" chores we have to do at home, school schedules, or appointments. This memory can be expanded as necessary.

Figure 47 is a drawing of a digital memory. As you can see, up to

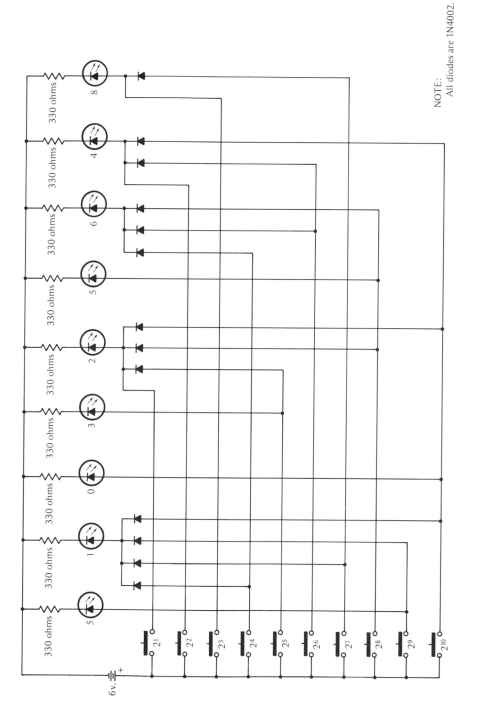

FIGURE 46   *Circuit diagram of powers-of-2 calculator.*

NOTE:
All diodes are 1N4002.

ten items are listed on the front panel. Five switches indicate the days of the week. Turning any one switch on will light the LED next to all of the items occurring that day. Items that occur on more than one day will be indicated on each of their days.

The circuit of the digital memory is shown in figure 48. As you can see, each item LED is connected to the output of a five diode OR gate. The number of inputs used for each gate depends on the number of days an item has to appear. If item 1 appears on Monday and Wednesday, for example, you would connect one of item 1's OR gate inputs to the Monday switch and one to the Wednesday switch. Connecting the inputs in this manner is a form of "hard-wire" programming. Figure 49 shows details of construction of an internal programming panel. By using such an arrangement for the gate inputs, you can easily reprogram by changing the various input switch wires with a screwdriver. The number of items can be expanded by adding an LED and OR gate for each additional item desired. If you wish to increase the number of days from five to seven, simply add two more diodes to each gate to form a seven-input OR gate.

FIGURE 47   *A digital memory.*

FIGURE 48

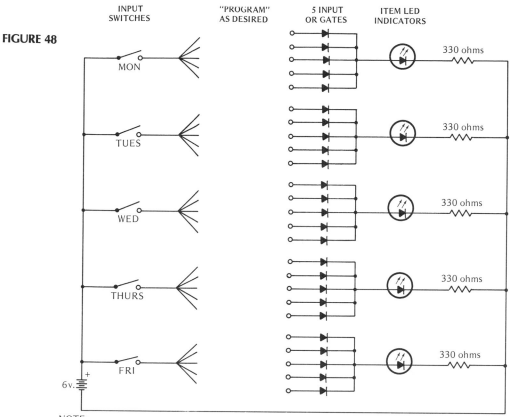

INPUT SWITCHES   "PROGRAM" AS DESIRED   5 INPUT OR GATES   ITEM LED INDICATORS

MON

TUES

WED

THURS

FRI

6v.

NOTE:
Only 5 indicators are shown for clarity. All others are connected in the same way.

Circuit of memory.

FIGURE 49   *A simple way to build a programming panel.*

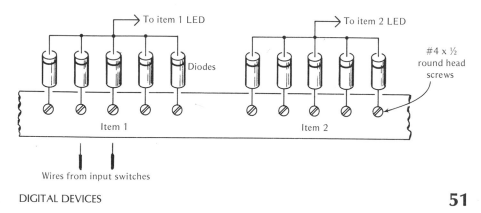

To item 1 LED

To item 2 LED

Diodes

#4 x ½ round head screws

Item 1

Item 2

Wires from input switches

DIGITAL DEVICES

CHAPTER 8

A logical
home-monitoring system

As the culmination of our discussion of logic circuits and their various applications, we will embark on an ambitious project in this chapter. This project will be a home-monitoring system that can check on the condition of windows and doors, room temperature, lights left on, water in the basement, and so on and can be expanded to a degree limited only by the imagination of the builder. The various parameters can also be switched between a monitor and alarm mode, thereby making the system quite flexible and versatile.

Figure 50 is a block diagram of two rooms of the monitor. As you can see, sensors located in a particular room are designated high-priority or low-priority, depending on their importance. Although each lights an indicator when activated, the high-priority sensors drive an OR gate that directly sounds an alarm when any one is activated. Low-priority sensors must be triggered in groups for an alarm condition to occur. These, therefore, drive AND gates. The output of the AND gates then drives the final OR gate, sounding the alarm.

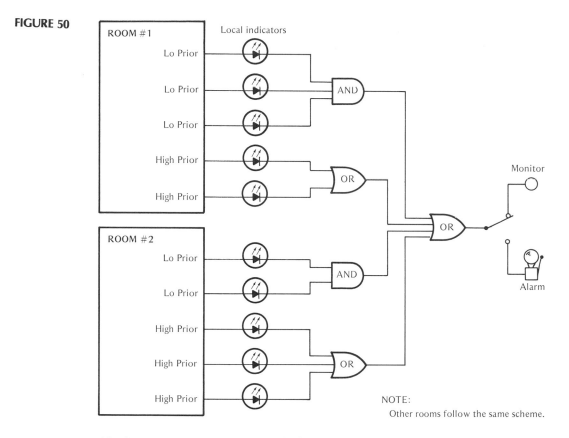

FIGURE 50

ROOM #1

Local indicators

Lo Prior
Lo Prior
Lo Prior

AND

High Prior
High Prior

OR

ROOM #2

Lo Prior
Lo Prior

AND

High Prior
High Prior
High Prior

OR

OR

Monitor

Alarm

NOTE:
Other rooms follow the same scheme.

Block diagram of two rooms of a home-monitoring system.

To begin, we must first build the sensors. These will be either open-circuit or closed-circuit, thereby producing logical 1's or 0's when activated. Figure 51 shows details of a simple window or door unit. It consists of an inexpensive pushbutton switch mounted in a tin can metal bracket and arranged so that closing the window or door activates the switch. Depending on the type of switch obtained, it may be open or closed circuit. An alternate method, shown in figure 52, is simply a bracket made of tin can metal that makes contact with two brass screws when the window or door is closed.

FIGURE 51

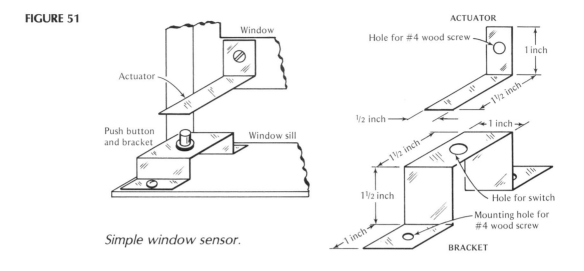

Simple window sensor.

Figure 53 is a sensing scheme that can be used to tell if an intruder passes a particular point. As you can see, it consists of two tin can metal contacts separated by a rectangular plastic card similar in size to a credit card. When someone disturbs the thread, the card is pulled from between the contacts and the circuit is completed.

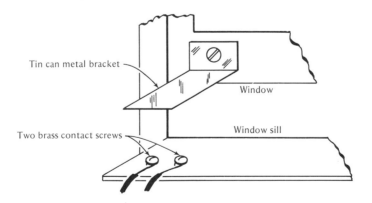

FIGURE 52   *Alternate window sensor.*

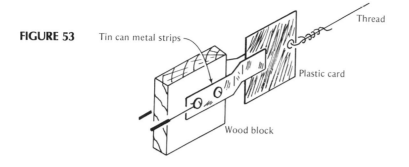

FIGURE 53

Tin can metal strips

Thread

Plastic card

Wood block

Intruder switch.

These sensors are both simple switches. The imaginative experimenter can devise many similar schemes to sense almost any type of movement. The following sensors are slightly more complex.

Figure 54 shows a simple water sensor. It consists of a thin piece of plastic upon which a layer of aluminum foil is glued with rubber cement (a). Carefully smooth the foil during gluing and, when the glue is dry, carefully cut out the flat pattern shown in (b) of the drawing with a hobby knife. Then mount the final assembly on a thin wood base (c). This sensor is used in conjunction with a transistor, as shown in figure 55, and will produce a logical 0 when even a small amount of water flows over the sensor.

Another transistor-related sensor is the light detector in figure 56. This sensor requires the purchase of a light-sensitive resistor, called a cadmium sulfide photocell or simply Cds photocell. This device, which usually costs only a dollar, passes a variable amount of current as a function of the amount of light falling on it. The transistor in the circuit in figure 56 will produce a logical 0 in the dark and a logical 1 in the light. Varying the position of the photocell will adjust the point at which the sensor switches.

A temperature sensor can be constructed with old thermostats, used to sense temperature in homes, which are often obtainable at no cost from local heating or air-conditioning dealers. These are either

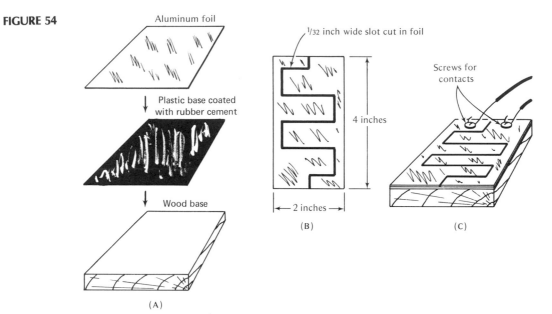

FIGURE 54

Aluminum foil

↓ Plastic base coated with rubber cement

Wood base

(A)

1/32 inch wide slot cut in foil

4 inches

2 inches

(B)

Screws for contacts

(C)

Mechanical details of water sensor.

open- or closed-circuit units and can be employed to monitor temperatures all around the house. In addition, any commercial fire- or burglar-alarm sensor can be employed with this system.

Once all of the sensors are built, it is time to start on the monitor unit. The enclosure for this unit is shown in figure 57. Actual size will

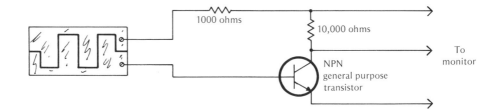

1000 ohms

10,000 ohms

NPN general purpose transistor

To monitor

FIGURE 55   *Electrical circuit of water sensor.*

FIGURE 56

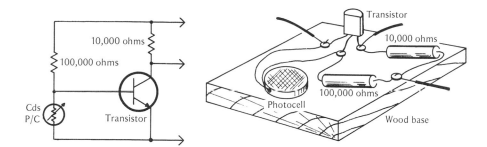

Light sensor details.

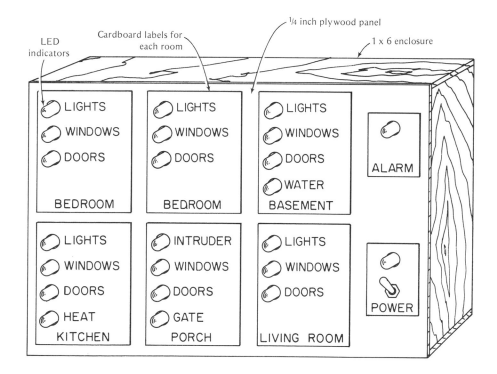

FIGURE 57   *Layout of monitoring system.*

depend on the number of sensors used, so exact dimensions are not shown. Before starting construction, however, read the entire chapter and decide how elaborate your monitor should be.

The monitor is divided into three sections: the input conditioner, which produces the correct logic for each sensor; the priority display selector, which is used to determine the ''importance'' of each input and display its status; and the actual alarm.

For the system to perform properly, all inputs must be logical 0 when not activated and logical 1 when activated. This means that the output of some sensors must be inverted. Figure 58 shows the circuit that will make up the input conditioner section. The number of inverting and noninverting circuits actually built will, of course, depend on the number of sensors used. Each sensor must have one or the other, however. Figure 59 shows how these input circuits are arranged at the bottom of the enclosure and how binder head wood screws are used with washers as input terminals.

Next the display portion should be laid out as in figure 60. Note that all gates are mounted on their own shelves, with wires from the input section neatly arranged as shown. When building this section try

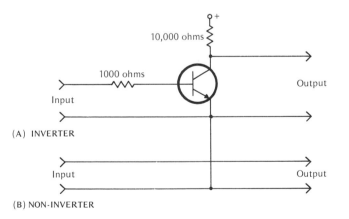

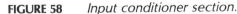

FIGURE 58   *Input conditioner section.*

FIGURE 59

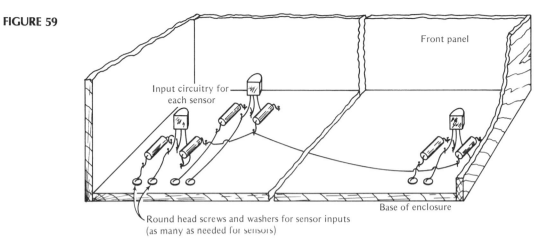

Input circuitry for each sensor

Front panel

Base of enclosure

Round head screws and washers for sensor inputs
(as many as needed for sensors)

Rear panel details.

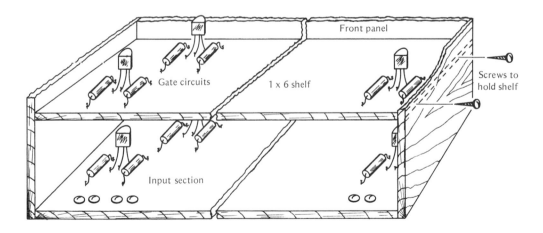

Gate circuits

1 x 6 shelf

Front panel

Screws to hold shelf

Input section

FIGURE 60   *Display section shelf.*

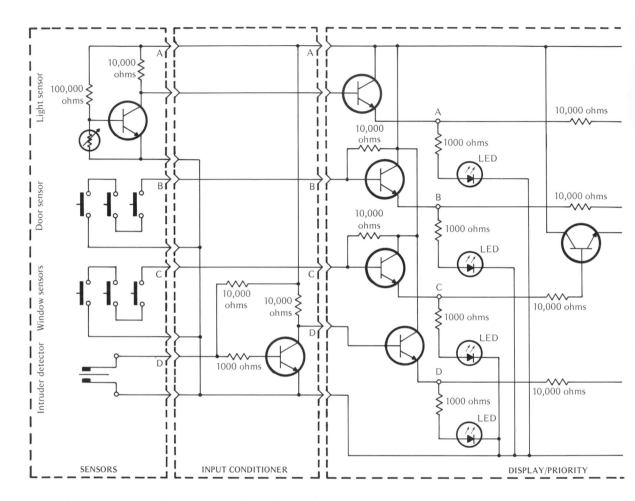

FIGURE 61   *Circuit of one room of monitoring system.*

to keep the location of the gates above the respective inputs. If you arrange the light-emitting diodes on the front panel, as shown in figure 57, a quick glance will show the status of the entire house. The LEDs, by the way, are of the same type as those used in chapter 7. The priority portion of this section consists of predominantly AND gates. These

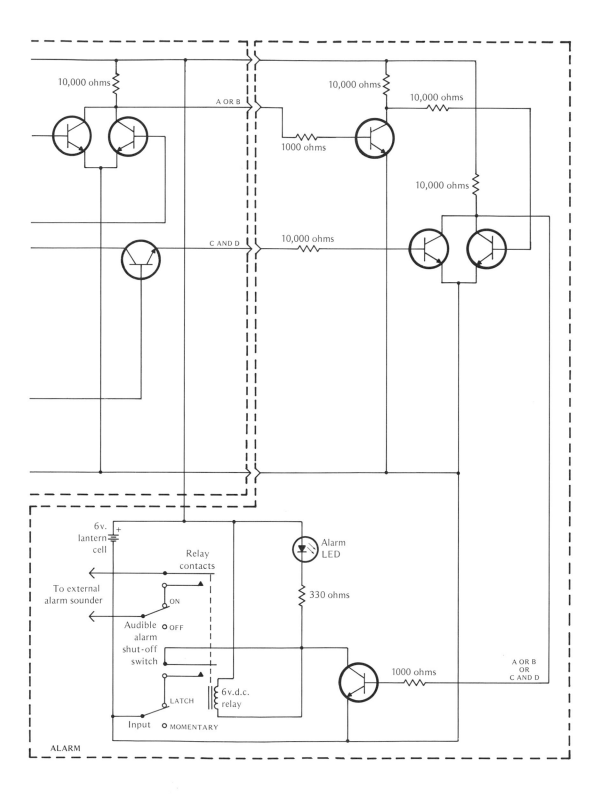

gates will, as previously mentioned, select combinations of sensors that have to be active in order for an alarm to sound. If you run out of room on the display shelf, you can build another shelf for the additional circuitry. Build enough AND gates to accommodate all the sensor combinations you want. When you have built this section, wait before making the final connections to the input conditioner section.

The final section consists of a single multiple-input OR gate and transistor-driven relay that can activate any alarm you desire. Fairly inexpensive burglar-alarm bells, sirens, or any other noisemaker can be employed, as well as floodlights if you wish. An audible alarm shutoff switch is also provided for convenience, as is a feature for momentary or continuous checking of the condition of each sensor.

Figure 61 shows a circuit of one room of a typical monitoring system. The one you build will, of course, be suited to your needs.

When everything is built, carefully check over all wiring. At this point the sections will be tested and connected together. We will start with the alarm section.

Apply power with the "audible alarm" switch off and the input switch to "momentary." Nothing should happen and no light should light. Using a second six-volt lantern battery, connect the − lead to the common point and the + lead to each input of the OR gate, one at a time. Each time you touch an input, the alarm LED should light and the relay "click" in. When this test is passed, set the input switch to "latch." Now when you touch that lead of the battery to an input, the alarm LED (and relay) should come on and stay on until you press the reset switch. In digital terms the circuit is said to have latched itself.

With the alarm section working, turn off the power and proceed to connect the priority display section. Again, turn on the power, return the input switch to momentary, and note that none of the LEDs nor the alarm LED is lit. Connect the battery to all gate inputs for a particular AND gate and check to be sure that the alarm LED goes on. When the LED goes on, the alarm relay should also click. Be sure that you test each AND gate in this manner. To test the OR gates, repeat the procedure with each input to an OR gate and be sure the alarm LED and relay operate.

Now remove power and connect the input conditioner circuits. Temporarily connect each input of this section individually to the common point for a normally low sensor, or directly to +6V for a normally high sensor. Apply power, and again no lamp or LED should light. Now move the lead from one sensor input at a time from common to +6, or vice versa, and check to be certain that the correct LED lights. When you are satisfied that each individual sensor input conditioner is working properly, remove a group that goes to an AND gate. The correct LEDs and the alarm lamp should now light. When this happens you are ready to test the sensors themselves.

Do this by connecting the +6V and common points to the sensors and a simple test indicator made of an LED and a resistor between the sensor output lead and common, as shown in figure 62. Apply power and look at the test indicator. A normally low sensor will cause the test LED to stay off, while a normally high sensor will cause it to go on. Activate each sensor and be sure that it works.

When all of these tests are completed, connect all of the sensors and activate each in turn as a final test. You are now ready to use the system.

You now have a monitor that is built along the lines of an actual computer-type device and that will prove a useful accessory to any home, from a simple apartment to a large mansion.

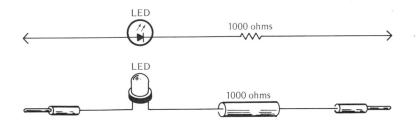

FIGURE 62   *Details of simple LED digital tester.*

CHAPTER 9

FUN AND GAMES

Most people are familiar with the wide variety of computer-controlled games that have appeared in recent years. These games, mostly digital in nature, are not different in principle from the circuits we have been using in the previous chapters. They are only more complex, often utilizing hundreds of thousands of components in integrated-circuit form and complex logic interconnections. While such circuits are beyond the scope of this book, there are several circuits and a complete game that can be easily built by the experimenter. All utilize techniques we have looked at before.

Figure 63 is a device employing logic circuitry that "automates" the familiar choosing game "Once, Twice, Shoot!" Here the idea is that two opponents, one "odd" and the other "even," put out one or two fingers at the command "shoot!" If both opponents put out the same number of fingers, the winner is odd. Three out of four wins the match.

In the electronic version, each player has two pushbuttons. One is "1" and other is "2," signifying the number of fingers. A small wooden barrier hides the opponents' pushbuttons from each other's view, while two LEDs indicate odd or even. Since construction details are quite straightforward, only overall dimensions are given. Details may be varied to suit the builder. Figure 64 is a circuit diagram of the unit. Wiring is straightforward and, for simplicity, four of the same type of pushbutton switches are used. Diode OR gates make certain that the correct light comes on. An advantage of the electronic circuit is that opponents must press their respective buttons before an LED comes on. Cheating, by waiting a split second after the opponent starts to make a move, is eliminated.

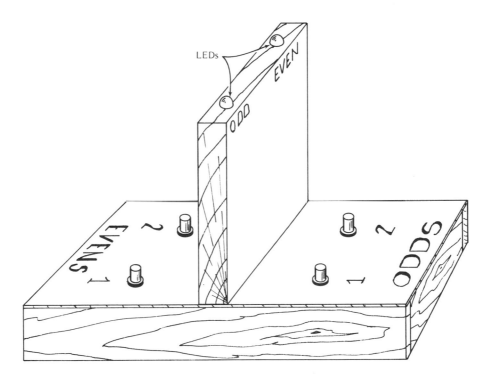

FIGURE 63 *"Once, Twice, Shoot!" game.*

FIGURE 64

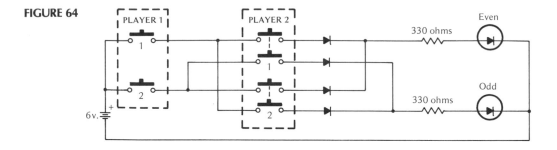

Circuit diagram of "Once, Twice, Shoot!"

Figure 65 shows an analog game called Threshold that can be played by two opponents in one of two ways. The first is to have one opponent set his knob to some point. The other opponent then tries to set his knob as close to the same point as possible without lighting the lamp or sounding the optional buzzer. After both opponents do this, the one who has come closer (determined by counting divisions between the set point and actual threshold) is the winner. In the second version the opponents take turns moving their knobs. The one who lights the lamp or sounds the buzzer first loses. Figure 66 is a circuit diagram of the game and, as you can see, consists of two potentiometers, both of which control the conduction of a transistor. In the circuit, when the two are set approximately 0.7 volts apart, this transistor conducts and two additional transistors activate the relay, sounding the buzzer and lighting the LED. Such a circuit is actually an analog (voltage) to digital (the lamp) converter and is often used with digital computers to allow them to process analog signals.

The games described both required two players. The one to follow tests the player against the machine.

There is an old game called Nim that has always been popular, particularly with young people. To play, two opponents alternately take 1,2,3, or 4 sticks from a pile of 21 until only one stick remains. The player who is forced to take the last stick is the loser. This game is fun to play and quite easy to "computerize." When you play the

FIGURE 65

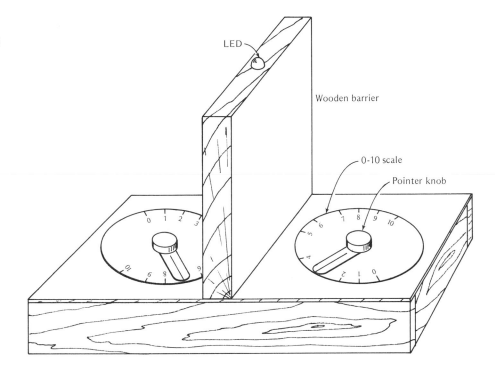

LED

Wooden barrier

0-10 scale

Pointer knob

Mechanical details of Threshold.

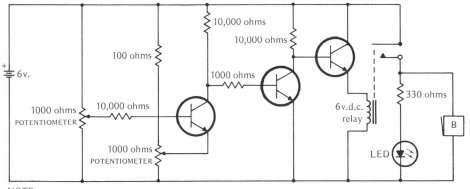

NOTE:
"B" is an optional 6 volt DC buzzer.

FIGURE 66   *Circuit diagram of Threshold.*

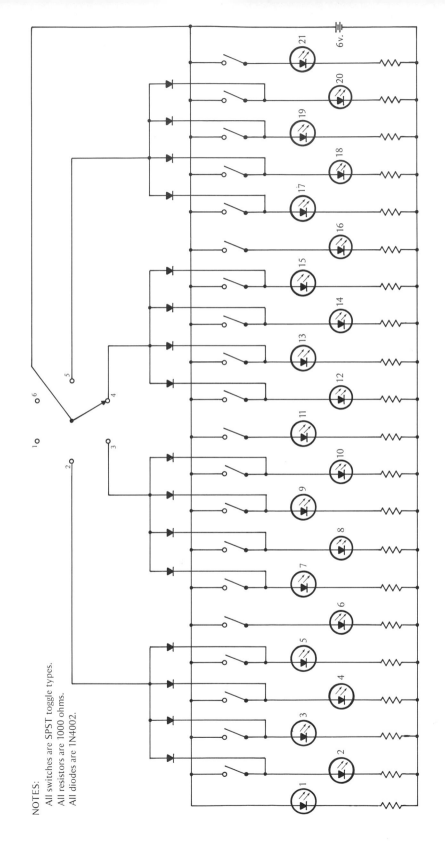

NOTES:

All switches are SPST toggle types.
All resistors are 1000 ohms.
All diodes are 1N4002.

FIGURE 67   *Circuit diagram of Nim.*

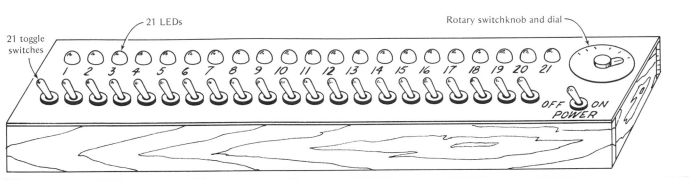

FIGURE 68   *Nim layout.*

computer, you can never win, since the circuitry never makes a mistake.

Figure 67 shows the complete circuit diagram of the game, while figures 68 and 69 show details of the cabinet and rotary switch wiring. All LEDs and diodes are the same as those used in earlier chapters. The 21 LEDs signify the sticks, and the 21 switches, the method for removing them. The six-position rotary switch and diode gate circuitry are the computer's memory. As you can see, the 21 LEDs are arranged in four groups of five. No matter how many LEDs are turned on by the human player, the machine responds by turning on the remaining LEDs in the group of five. The last two positions of the rotary switch are

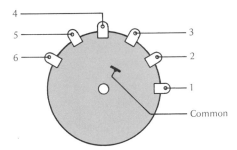

FIGURE 69   *Rear view of common rotary switch.*

simply to confuse the player. Therefore, the human player (if he or she goes first) must always turn on the last LED and lose. To play the game, all LED switches are turned off and the "computer's move" switch is turned to position #1. Starting from left to right, the machine's opponent turns on one, two, three, or four LEDs. The computer's move switch is then turned to position #2, and the circuit makes its move. The game continues in this manner until the last LED is illuminated. Although the winning principle is easy to figure out from the circuit, playing the game is fun, and newcomers will be amazed at the "skill" of the machine.

The three games described may not have the excitement of what is normally thought of as a computer-controlled game, but they should illustrate some of the fun ways circuitry can be used. When you gain an understanding of what it really does and how the concepts are related to play, there is no limit to the types of games you can devise. For example, game 1 could also be two space invaders blasting each other with laser weapons, game 2, deactivating a nuclear power plant, and game 3, destroying enemy missiles while the enemy destroys yours. It depends only on how you look at it.

CHAPTER 10

MODERN COMPUTERS

Modern computers and calculators, although using many of the techniques and circuits described in the previous chapters, are vastly more complex. Utilizing digital logic techniques, many integrated circuits containing thousands of transistors are interconnected in complex arrays that do the actual computing. Because the circuitry is so complex and the intended operators of these computers are nontechnical personnel, the various computer elements are arranged in ways that allow such people to have some overall idea of their organization.

Figure 70 is a photograph of a modern computer, and figure 71 is a block diagram of its main components. Input devices such as typewriterlike keyboards, pushbuttons, and even special magnetic tape recorders are employed to give instructions to the computer. Because of the complexity of the circuitry, all interconnections are made by the computer. Communicating is by means of a code called a language, which the operator feeds into the machine. This language tells the

FIGURE 70

A typical small computer for use in the home.

computer what to do and in what order. Instructions in this special language are typed into the machine on a typewriter keyboard or other input device. This process is called programming. The entire program is then stored in the memory section for future use. When a complete set of instructions or a program is to be used, the operator indicates this on the keyboard. The central processing unit or CPU then rearranges and reconnects the circuitry within the machine to follow the programmed instructions. Results of the computations are indicated on an output device that may be a television-type screen, called a CRT, or a printer that produces a permanent record.

As intelligent and clever as the computer may seem, it still does

FIGURE 71

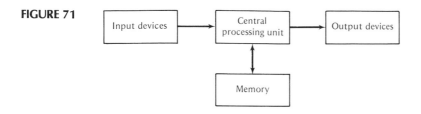

Block diagram of a modern computer.

only what it has been instructed to do, a fact we have emphasized before. This is true even with the most complex of the modern machines. By way of example, let us look at figure 72.

This is a copy of an actual program that could be typed directly onto the keyboard of a computer. While very simple as programs go, it is similar in style to many of the programs in use today. This particular program is written in a computer language called BASIC, which is just one of a number of currently used languages and will serve to illustrate our point.

The number to the left of each statement indicates the order in

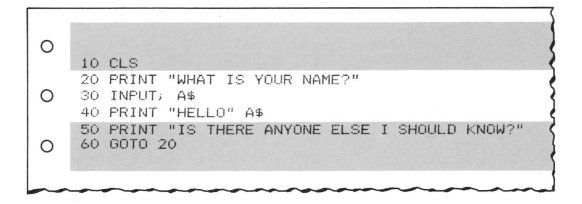

FIGURE 72   *Simple computer program.*

which the computer will look at each line. Normally, space is left between lines for the insertion of additional statements as the program is modified. That is why the lines are numbered in steps of ten. You would add a line between 10 and 20, for example, by calling it 15. The entry on line 10 means "clear screen." This tells the computer to erase all writing on the CRT screen, making it blank. Line 20 tells the computer to print on the screen the words within the quotation marks, "What is your name?" The next line, you will notice, is an input. When the computer sees an input statement, it looks for data. In this case the data would be your name, and the computer would tag it with the abbreviation A$. In BASIC language, a letter followed by a dollar sign usually signifies a string of up to 256 characters. For ease in computation the computer works only with A$, instead of all the characters.

Line 40 tells the computer to print "Hello," then the string of letters corresponding to your name. Reading the screen makes you think the computer actually knows you, but of course, it is only responding to the program. If you were to enter the word "automobile" when it asked for your name, the computer would print "Hello, automobile." Line 50 asks another question, and then line 60 immediately reverts to line 20.

If you enter another name, the A$ string will change to correspond to the new name and the program will repeat. In fact, as long as you add names, the computer will repeat its one-track message over and over again. By clever programming you can see that the computer could be made to say almost anything.

Although computers are becoming more and more familiar and important in our lives, we are living at the beginning of this amazing new technology. As time goes on the computer will surely play an ever-growing role in much of what we do — from games for enjoyment to tools in our very jobs and lives. By having some understanding of what really goes on, we can accept this marvel for what it really is — an electronic device that can help make our lives easier and more enjoyable.

Index